ALLIGATOR FARMS

FUNKY FARMS

Lynn M. Stone

The Rourke Corporation, Inc.
Vero Beach, Florida 32964

PHOTO CREDITS:
All photos © Lynn M. Stone

ACKNOWLEDGMENT:
The author thanks Allan Register and Gatorama, Palmdale, Florida, for their cooperation and assistance in the preparation of this book.

EDITORIAL SERVICES:
Susan Albury

CREATIVE SERVICES:
East Coast Studios, Merritt Island, Florida

Library of Congress Cataloging-in-Publication Data

Stone, Lynn M.
    Alligator farms / by Lynn M. Stone
        p. cm. — (Funky farms)
    Summary: Describes the physical characteristics and habits of alligators and how they are raised in captivity on farms in southern states.
    ISBN 0-86593-538-6
    1. Alligator farming Juvenile literature. 2. American alligator Juvenile literature. [1. Alligators. 2. Alligator farming.] I. Title. II. Series: Stone, Lynn M. Funky farms.
SF515.5.A44S76 1999
639.3'98—dc21   99-25277
                                                                                    CIP

Printed in the USA

CONTENTS

ALLIGATORS

Alligators look like giant lizards. They have leathery skin, long tails, and wide, toothy jaws.

Like lizards, alligators are **reptiles** (REP tilz). Snakes and turtles are also reptiles.

All reptiles are cold-blooded. That means their bodies stay about the same temperature as the air or water around them. Alligators often lie on riverbanks or shorelines on cool days. By sunning themselves, the gators warm up.

A big gator crawls from an alligator farm pond onto shore. The alligator will lie on the bank and sun itself.

Alligators live in the swamps, ponds, and rivers of the southern states. They are excellent swimmers. They eat anything they can catch in the water. Most of their **prey** (PRAY), however, are turtles or fish.

Alligators can live for many years and become quite large. The biggest gators can measure over 10 feet (3 meters) long.

Alligators are closely related to crocodiles and the **caimans** (KAY munz) of South America.

Wild alligators live largely on a diet of turtles and fish. This adult farm gator is growing on a diet of chicken.

ALLIGATOR FARMS

Swamps in the South aren't the only places to find gators. They're also found on alligator farms.

People who raise large numbers of alligators in **captivity** (kap TIV uh tee) are alligator farmers. Alligator farmers earn money by raising gators for their meal and their **hides** (HIDEZ), or skins. Some gator farmers also sell alligator skulls and feet as souvenirs.

Many alligator farms are open to the public. Visitors can see hundreds of alligators at close range.

An alligator farmer rolls a fresh alligator hide in salt. Salt protects the hide from spoiling until it reaches a tannery.

9

WHERE ALLIGATOR FARMS ARE

Alligators need warm weather to remain active and healthy. As a result, alligator farms are in many of the same states where alligators live in the wild.

Louisiana has more alligator farms than any other state. A big Louisiana farm can produce 70,000-80,000 alligator skins each year.

Other states with alligator farms are Florida, Georgia, North Carolina, Texas, Mississippi, and Alabama.

On a warm, sunny day, farm gators in Florida meet under palmetto leaves.

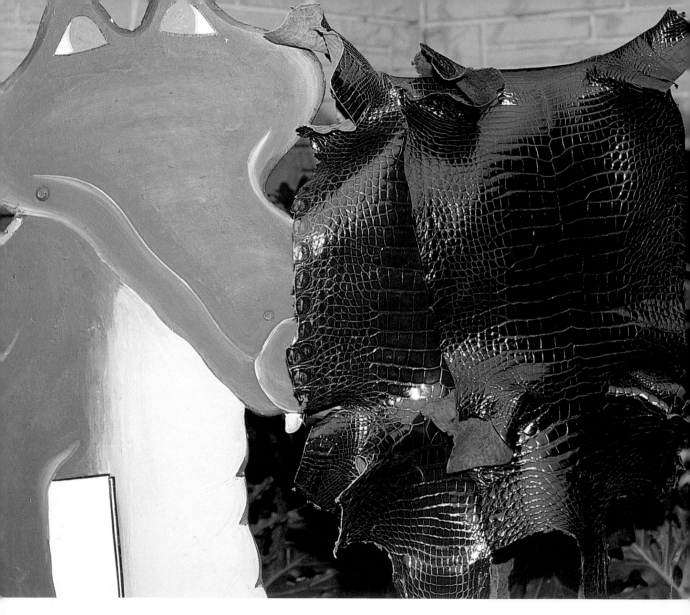

Alligator hides like these are dyed. They will be turned into leather products.

A baby alligator frees itself from the egg that was its home for 60 days.

RAISING ALLIGATORS

How much land—and water— an alligator farmer needs depends upon several things. For instance, not all gator farms have alligators that build nests and lay eggs.

If a farmer wants his or her gators to nest on the farm, the alligators need a big pond with plenty of wild plants. The female gator makes her nest—a big mound—of plant stems and leaves.

Young gators splash in the pen of their "grow-out" house. The water can be drained easily for cleaning the pen.

Alligator farmers buy at least some alligator eggs. In Florida, for example, gator farmers can buy the eggs of wild alligators for about $9 each from the state. The state of Florida makes sure that not too many eggs in any one area are taken from the wild.

The farmer keeps alligator eggs in an **incubator** (INK u bay tur) for about 60 days. Afterward, the baby gators are put into a "grow-out" house where they have sunlight and water. The water is kept warm, and the gators feed once daily.

Alligator eggs stay toasty on the shelf of an incubation house, or incubator.

By the time they're two years old, the farm gators are from four and a half to five feet (1.4-1.5 meters) long. Then they're **butchered** (BUHT churd), or killed, for their meat and skin.

The farmer rolls the gator hide in salt to help it dry out and cure. After about four days of salt curing, the hide is sent to a **tannery** (TAN nur ee).

A tannery makes animal hides into fine leather. It may also dye the hide a new color.

Alligator leather is used in shoes, belts, key cases, and other products.

WHY ALLIGATORS?

Both alligator hides and meat are valuable. Alligator leather is soft, but very tough. The squarish markings in the skin give alligator hide a special look.

Alligator leather can be finished to look shiny or rather dull.

A five-foot (1.5 meters) gator skin is worth about $90 before it's made into a belt, jacket, wallet, or shoes.

Alligator meat is in greater demand than alligator hides. The meat sells for up to $10 per pound ($22 per kilogram).

Fresh, frozen alligator meat is sold in many southern markets.

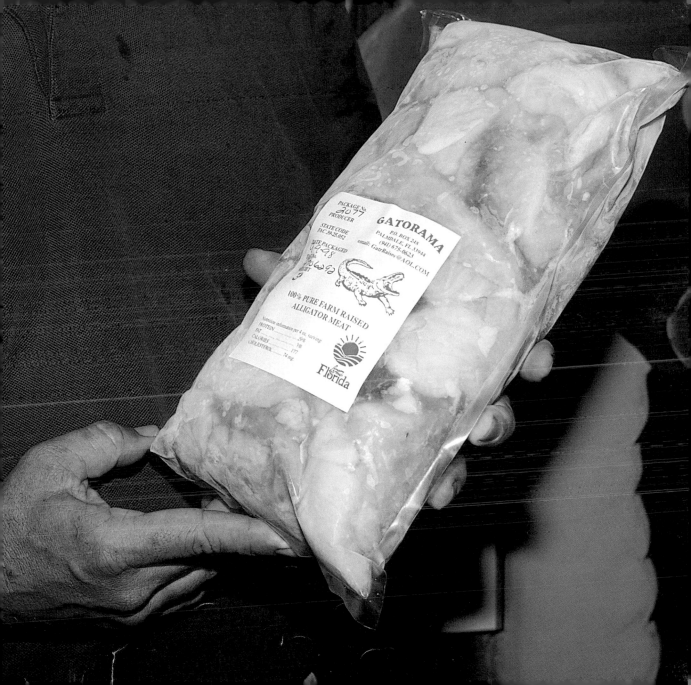

ALLIGATOR FARMS IN THE FUTURE

Alligator farmers will probably continue to see a high demand for gator steaks. It's not unusual in Florida, for example, to see alligator meat on restaurant menus.

The market for alligator leather may be weaker. The problem that alligator farmers face is look-alike leather. Many nations sell cowhide that looks like alligator. Since cowhide is cheaper to buy, many people are happy with the look-alike product.

Leather makers can make cowhide look like alligator by pressing gator hide shapes into it.

GLOSSARY

butchered (BUHT churd) — to have been killed, or slaughtered, for meat and other human uses

caiman (KAY mun) — a close, South American cousin of the alligator

captivity (kap TIV uh tee) — the holding of an animal behind fences or caging of some kind; a place where an animal is held by people

hide (HIDE) — the skin of an animal

incubator (INK u bay tur) — an instrument or place that keeps eggs or baby animals continually warm

prey (PRAY) — an animal that is killed by other animals for food

reptile (REP til) — the group of animals including snakes, lizards, turtles, and the tuatara; cold-blooded, air-breathing animals with scaly skins or shells

tannery (TAN nur ee) — a place where animal hides are tanned or otherwise colored

INDEX

FURTHER READING

Find out more about alligators with these helpful books and information sites:

Chatfield, June. *A Look Inside Reptiles.* Joshua Morris, 1995
McCarthy, Colin. *Reptile.* Knopf, 1991
Stone, Lynn. *Alligators and Crocodiles.* Children's Press, 1989

Florida Department of Agriculture on line at fl-ag.com (follow alligator link).